ow to use the stickers

Look out for pai[...] you bought this [...] for under Loo[...] e right number of [...]

Score 5 f[...] people enjoying the[...]

Score 15 for a painting of people enjoying themselves in winter

Score 5 for a painting of a scary storm

Score 10 for a painting of a saint

Score 20 for a painting of a saint with a devil or dragon

Score 15 for a painting of a noisy city scene

Score 10 for a painting of a noisy battle scene

Score 20 for a painting of people making music

GW01367507

Wame

What a laugh!

Can you spot people having a great time on the ice? Imagine the sound of laughing, shouting – and crying when they fell over!

A Winter Scene with Skaters near a Castle by Hendrick Avercamp. Find out more on page 1.

Hendrick Avercamp was born in the Netherlands, a very flat country. When ndrick was alive, over 400 years ago, the untryside near his home often flooded and ze over in the winter. People living there arnt to ice skate when they were very ung. What other activities can you spot ople doing on the ice?

Lookout!

Look out for paintings of people enjoying themselves. Score extra for people enjoying themselves in winter. Find out what you score on page 2.

Little boy
Pair of skates
Hole in the ice-
Pearly gates

Hendrick couldn't hear or speak. So although he painted people chattering, laughing and shouting, his own world was silent.

A scary storm

Imagine you're in a jungle, in a thunderstorm. The wind howls, trees groan, rain beats down and thunder cracks overhead. A tiger growls nearby . . .

Detail from *Tiger in a Tropical Storm(Surprise* by Henri Rousseau. Find out more on page 1.

Would you be scared if you met this tiger? Do you think the artist once saw tiger in the jungle? Or did he make this cture up?

The artist Henri Rousseau told everyone that he had seen a tiger in a jungle. But the tiger is probably copied from a picture in a book. Henri probably painted the jungle after visiting botanical gardens in France where he lived.

People said that Henri frightened himself by looking at his own jungle paintings!

Lookout!

Look out for paintings of scary storms. They don't have to be in a jungle – it could be at sea or in the countryside. Find out what you score on page 2.

Screams or squeaks?

Saint Michael is about to kill the devil. The devil looks as though it is pleading for mercy. Is it hissing like a snake? Or squeaking like a bat?

Part of the fun of painting a devil is that you can draw what you like. In the mid-1500s, when this picture was made, artists drew devils as a mixture of snakes, birds an dragons. What creatures do you use when drawing monsters or aliens? Dinosaurs? Lizards? Bats?

This little devil doesn't look very scary, does it? It looks more like a naughty imp. Saint Michael looks as though he wants to teach it a lesson rather than kill it. What do you think?

Look out for paintings of saints. Score extra for a saint with a devil or a dragon. Find out what you score on page 2.

Lookout!

Detail from *Saint Michael triumphant over the Devil with the Donor Antonio Juan* by Bartolomé Bermejo. Find out more on page 1.

an old saying:

If I lie and do you wrong
May the devil split my tongue

Hissing steam

Steam trains, like the ones in this picture, hissed loudly when engines let off steam. People waiting on the platform jumped out of their skins!

The Gare St-Lazare by Claude Monet. Find out more on page 1.

he artist, Claude Monet, lived near this railway station in Paris. He tried to ow what the noise of trains, jostling ople and the smoky atmosphere felt e. Do you think he succeeded? Claude inted twelve different pictures of -Lazare in different weather and at fferent times of the year.

Lookout!

Look out for paintings of noisy city scenes. Find out what you score on page 2.

Claude painted quickly to catch the changing light and atmosphere. A hundred years ago, when *The Gare St-Lazare* was painted, most people liked pictures that looked as if they had been painted very carefully over a long time. People weren't used to paintings that looked as though they had been done quickly. When Claude showed his pictures at an exhibition, people said they were rubbish. Today, they sell for millions of pounds!

ction man!

What noises would you have heard on a battlefield in the past? Whinnying horses? Shouting? The clash of swords?

Banastre Tarleton was a British hero in the American War of Independence, 200 years ago. Later Colonel Tarleton had his portrait painted. He wanted to be seen as a man of action. So Sir Joshua Reynolds, who painted this picture, included horses, flags and smoke.

What happened to the karate rt who joined e army?

He saluted and nearly k... him

Colonel Tarleton lost two fingers in battle. But Sir Joshua painted his hand so that we can't see his missing fingers.

Don't worry it's not loaded!

Lookout!

Look out for paintings of noisy battle scenes. Find out what you score on page 2.

Detail from *Colonel Banastre ...rleton* by Sir Joshua ...nolds. Find out more on page 1.

Making music

This picture was probably painted to decorate a room. The young man in the centre sings and plays a lute (a stringed instrument a bit like a guitar). The other two sing and beat time. Can you spot the fiddle, a recorder and a music book?

What's a cat's favourite musical instrument?

A mouse organ!

Detail from *A Concert* by Lorenzo Costa. Find out more on page 1.

When you get home . . .

Lookout!

Look out for paintings showing people making music. Find out what you score on page 2.

. . . make an ELASTIC BAND LUTE.

Collect several elastic bands of different thicknesses. Stretch them over an empty tissue box leaving a gap of about 1 cm between each one. Cut two pieces of wood about 1 cm square and as wide as the box. Place one at each end of the box, between the bands and the box. You should be able to play a simple tune.

Ask a grown-up to help you cut the wood!

. . . that in the Middle Ages artists drew devils as a mixture of snakes, birds and dragons?

. . . that one artist was afraid of his own paintings? Inside you'll find more fantastic facts, STICKERS, jokes and how to make a noisy ELASTIC BAND LUTE!

Lookout! guides to collect now

- Castles
- Paintings
- Abbeys & Cathedrals

collect Lookout! guides

Why not put all your LOOKOUT! guides in a brilliant LOOKOUT! binder costing £6.50 (inc. p&p to UK address). Write to Pitkin Unichrome, Healey House, Dene Road, Andover, Hants SP10 2AA. Phone 01264 409206; fax 01264 334110; or email: guides@pitkin-unichrome.com

ISBN 0-85372-971-9

9 780853 729716

£ 0.50

shouting